EPISODES OF LIVING

EPISODES OF LIVING

By Helen Stayton Persse

With quotations by her late father,
Playwright and dramatist, Frank Stayton

© Copyright 2002
By Helen Stayton Persse

© Copyright 2002
The Stayton Trust

All rights reserved.

The use or reproduction of this work in any form, electronic or mechanical, or other means now known or hereafter invented, including photocopying and recording, and in any information storage and retrieval system is forbidden without the written permission of the author.

ISBN N0.: 0 9541256 0

Published in Toronto, Canada, by Stayton Publishing
First Publish Date August 2002

Printed in Toronto, Canada, by Foster Printing

Illustrations by Michael B

DEDICATION

I dedicate this small book to my three children ...
to Peter for his encouragement, to Michael whose vision and perception match my own and who has spent many hours in researching photographs, and designing the layout, and to my daughter Antonia, whose endless patience in helping me with editing poems and putting them onto the computer has made this anthology possible.

Also to my late father, whose love of freedom and truth were paramount to his way of life, superseding his material success in his writing.

Helen Stayton Persse

Helen Persse

I have known Helen Persse since 1996 when she moved to England from Canada and came to live in Woodbridge, Suffolk. In these latter years she has sought and found the freedom to reflect on her life and to express her inner experiences through prose and poetry. She has faced many vicissitudes of childhood and adulthood, often on her own, and from these she has learned independence, strength and determination, yet retained and sometimes hidden her inner gentler needs. Her writing well portrays some of the conflicts and confluences of her inner and outer lives.

To have completed this book against all the odds of failing eyesight necessitating magnifying visual aids, and a dense right sided hemiplegia (paralysis) with the loss of her right hand, not to mention the usual hazards of printing and publishing, is a quite remarkable achievement.

Dr. Ian Leith (May 25 2002)

INTRODUCTION

I have tried to make this collection of poems, prose, incidents and short stories varied. The highs and lows of a strange upbringing and life, as the third child of a dramatist and author. I was a loner and a rebel – my only education being the vicissitudes of life in London, the country, France and the Middle East. A life devoted to my children and also to teaching dyslexic children for many years.

The yearning to write was, I think, always with me; as was searching for a soul mate and some roots – some of my poems portray this.

Now I am trying to catch up with my life in a wheel-chair - after working until 1994; time spent in Canada, and finally having to sell my home in Woodbridge after suffering a right-sided stroke and having to teach myself to write with my left hand.

Helen Stayton Persse

TABLE OF CONTENTS

Episodes of Living	1
Moments of Loving	3
Reflections	5
Earth's Injustice	6
The Mystery of Life	7
A Cottage in the Country	8
Love on a Railway Train (Short Story)	9
Memories—Canada	11
The White House	12
The Old Cottage	13
Memories of Iraq	15
Basra	16
Memories of Dubai	17
Thoughts of Living	18
Memories	19
A Drive Across the Desert (Short Story)	20
Emotions	22
Moods	23
Conflict	24
Night	25
Happiness	26

TABLE OF CONTENTS

Time, What is Time ?	27
Waiting, a Gift of Time	28
A Stranger from Afar	29
Where are we Going ?	30
Seasons	32
Spring	33
Solitude	35
In Limbo	36
Thoughts Lying on a Hospital Bed	37
View from my Window	38
On Coming to Terms with Life	39
Good Friday	40
Freesias	41
A Changing Direction (Short Story)	42
Children	48
My Children	49
Bear (Short Story)	50
Reincarnation	52
Blackout	54
Finding the Way	55
Philosophies of Living—Being	57

Love isn't just ..... desire. It's the greatest form of self-expression, without self coming into it ...
F.S

EPISODES OF LIVING

To live is to reach the heights
And the depths;
The goodness of people
In close relationships.
Moments of supreme happiness
And fulfilment ...
But what _is_ happiness?
A few fleeting moments.
The warmth of unity
In speaking the same language.
To live is to suffer.
To know the depths of despair;
Uncertainty, black depression
That can easily engulf one.
Perhaps these moments of visions
Of supreme happiness
Are purely a preparation
For an eventual haven -
When life's obstacles
Are finally overcome.
To live is to feel,
To be aware of sound and smell
And the beauty and harshness .....cont.

...... *Episodes of living*

Of nature – the song of birds.
An exquisite melody.
Painters, writers, musicians
Lived for their creativeness,
Suffering deprivation.
And yet, with their sufferings
Have left a richness to help mankind.
This is the constant cycle of life.
Fulfilment of living
Is to be fortunate in meeting
A soul-mate whose awareness
Is akin to one's own.
Seldom achieved in one lifetime ...

MOMENTS OF LOVING

The joy of knowing he comes to see you
With only an hour to spare before departure.
The final embrace, the passionate loving
And need to relax with one another.

Time - always time (the 'plane leaves in less
Than an hour and we must not sleep).
We kiss goodbye (when do I see you again?)
He has gone - no way of communicating.

A day goes by - a week;
You wonder whether it was a figment of the imagination ...
This rapture of living and loving
Sharing our thoughts - our love of life.

Dancing - with our love of rhythm and absolute timelessness.
Able to be oneself - completely relaxed.
To love - to give and to share, is fulfilment of living,
So seldom possible to achieve ..... Cont.

..... moments of loving

Another week goes by ...
You wonder whether it is worth giving and loving,
When too often it is followed by uncertainty
And an overwhelming emptiness.

Here – in this remote part of the Middle East,
When loneliness and depression is forever at your door,
Life seems to stand still – except for brief periods
Of glorious living.

Always, it seems, one meets people who speak
The same language.
A feeling of security and happiness;
You know it is but a fleeting time of peace.

"Ships that pass in the night!"

Page 4

REFLECTIONS

True love is a rare quality
Seldom achieved in a lifetime.
Yet a meeting of kindred souls
Who have the same visions –
And the same perceptions
Is a wondrous gift.
Meetings may be short
But the de is cast.
Life will never be the same;
The longing to share one's thoughts,
The touch of a hand,
A gentle kiss …
Perhaps we will meet
In another life.
Better to remain a loner,
To dream, perhaps,
Of what life could be
In another age – another time … .

EARTH'S INJUSTICE

Earth's injustice ... why?
Man's inhumanity to man;
The world's axis
Seems to move too fast!
The greater the speed
The greater man's greed.
Envy of power
Of those who prosper.

Murder, drug dealings, theft
And other monstrous crimes –
Regardless of retribution
In the days to come.
Earth's injustice ...
Earthquakes and hurricanes,
Floods and other disasters
Throughout the civilized world.

Time has become our enemy.
All over the world
Our senses have become cloudy.
No time to behold
Wonders of the world
Timeless and eternal.
What has happened to man's soul?
To his sense of feeling, seeing?

Awareness of the world around him ...
We must give back
Something of ourselves –
Before it is too late.

THE MYSTERY OF LIFE

There are many episodes of living. Is there a pattern?
Do we transgress from one way of life to another
Until peace and fulfilment is reached?
Imagery – reality?
We imagine how we'd _like_ our lives to be ...
Sometimes we get lost and take the wrong turning
With many ups and downs,
Before we are once more on an even keel.

I believe we are all born with dual personalities, a blend of genes from
both parents.
Which becomes the strongest depends on environment or upbringing.
But will we ever know?
It takes many years to find our true selves ...
How many are unable to find their souls? Who take to the road of evil –
Of murder and other monstrous crimes of this modern age.
They were babies once.
They had families and love. What happened to them?
The evil drug barons, those with sick minds
Whose only interest is destruction.
What happened to their childhood, their family life,
Their hope for the future?

A new millennium – a new century!
Retribution, perhaps, for those whose life is evil.
Evil is the devil and leads to misery.
Whereas God is good, and goodness creates peace of mind
And a tranquil way of life.
A dream, perhaps, of how life could be ...
The beauty around us - the simple things of life.
No matter how hard life can be, let us look outwards ...

A COTTAGE IN THE COUNTRY

Spiders – cobwebs of yesteryear;
Leaded windows and cracked panes.
A stove of unknown vintage;
Cracks on the walls,
Plaster falling off.
Will the windows open?
The garden is a wilderness
Where once roses grew.
A fig tree grows up the frontage –
Untouched by man.
Dead trees abound;
Firewood for the open grate,
But will the chimney smoke?
Disturbing bird's nests.

After negotiating pot-holes
Along the winding drive,
There is an air of remoteness.
Sheep and cattle graze nearby.
Far away from the noise
And bustle of highways,
The town but a few miles away.
A far cry from the uniformity
Of modern living ...
When the dust of ages is swept away,
The floor scrubbed
And the cottage is once more
A home and haven.
There will be peace!

LOVE ON A RAILWAY TRAIN

I was working as a teacher in a small school in a village in Kent – travelling the opposite way to daily commuters, an asset as it gave me time to read and to catch up with myself, after seeing my children off to school.

On Wednesdays I took a train home at about one o'clock ... always at this time was a stranger, a man going to London. It became habitual for us to chat and share the same carriage and, I must confess, I looked forward to his company and stimulating conversation. An enigmatic personality; he had strong, fine hands that were used to working on the land, perhaps. In our short journey together, maybe half an hour, the depth of our conversation and feelings grew stronger – and yet I knew so little about him.

This strange romance continued for some months but I had to tell him that I was getting married for the second time, to an older man who offered me security but for whom I had no love. As the day of this marriage drew nearer our mutual feelings nearly overwhelmed me – he begged me to 'run away' with him. My duty to my three children was too strong, however, and we said goodbye. *Cont.*

.... Love on a railway train

This was not the end of the story. He knew where I was living and used to leave notes on the windscreen of my car – to say he would attune his mind to mine at a certain time in the evening – especially on a clear and moonlit night. The closeness of our minds was a little frightening.

The notes and telephone calls ceased suddenly – which caused me great anguish ... then a call to say he'd had an accident and had been in hospital.

It took a long time to get this haunting personality out of my system and was not conducive to happy family life. Perhaps it was a figment of the imagination ... who knows?

The End.

MEMORIES OF CANADA

Camping beside the lake in Canada

A campsite amidst pine trees;
The sound of gently rippling water
By the lake.

The view breathtaking in its stark beauty.
Chipmunks dart around, hunting for food.
Loons can be heard, echoing across the lakes...

An eerie sound, as they call to their mates.
Racoons scavenge among trash bins
Scattering rubbish, scraps and tins.

And in some remote area
There's danger from prowling bears.
The smell of campfires as darkness descends;
There is magic in the sounds and smells.
The harshness and beauty of the night
As we sit around our campfire ...
The burning logs give us light.

THE WHITE HOUSE

The White House was over a century old,
Outwardly appearing rather stark and cold.
It stood near the end of a wide highway
Of a small township in Ontario ...
Called 'A Village in a City'.
Within the house a large open room,
A vast fireplace for burning logs.
A wide wooden stairway
With a balcony above,
And small rooms with ill-fitting doors.
Bats would appear from no-one knew where;
It was said that ghosts might appear!
The kitchen looked on to a large backyard;
The trees were huge, with exotic birds.
At the end of the grounds was the railway;
Long-distance trains with endless trucks.
A deck or patio on a raised platform
Where meals could be eaten in the glorious sun.
But very bleak in the winter snow.
The house was a haven for teenagers and cats,
Who slept in the basement, regardless of bats!
It was a strange house.

THE OLD COTTAGE

A young couple – fairly recently married, decide to move out of London to an old cottage in the country. John is a writer and Maria is a free-lance artist. They fall in love with their new dwelling, in spite of its lack of modern amenities, and soon have it habitable.

They begin to quarrel over names for their coming baby – both suffering from the traumas of such a major upheaval.

John loses himself in his work but Maria is restless and a little worried about her first unborn child. One night she goes to bed earlier than usual, the quarrel about naming the baby uppermost in her mind; she is aware of a strange atmosphere and sounds, almost of moaning. She rushes downstairs screaming but John tells her not to be childish and continues with his writing. Maria returns to their bedroom and buries her head under the pillow until John comes to bed.

The next night the same thing happens but the moaning seems to be louder; she again rushes downstairs but catches her foot on the rather old stair-carpet, falling down several stairs. John leaps from his chair, rushing to her aid, but she doesn't appear to be breathing. He carries her to the couch and then telephones for an ambulance, worried both for her health and that of their unborn child.

As Maria recovers in hospital, suffering only from shock and a few bruised bones, they are both reassured that the baby is all right. John is very upset and promises never to have such stupid quarrels again and they are both laughing and crying. .... Cont.

... the old cottage

Meanwhile, during Maria's stay in hospital, John goes to the estate agent to try to find more details of the history of the cottage .....
It seems that a young couple lived there several centuries ago. Her husband bullied her until one day, in despair, she pushed him down the stairs and he was killed. The wife was so filled with remorse that she killed herself and has haunted the cottage ever since; but only if there is disharmony. Those who live a reasonably peaceful life there will not be aware of this poor, haunted spirit and will be left in peace.
John told this story to Maria and they vowed to live in harmony for the rest of their lives.

John became a successful writer and, with their four children, they lived a full and happy life in the cottage for many, many years.

The End

MEMORIES OF BASRA, IRAQ

Date palms
Wild dogs
Primitive dwellings
And chickens scrubbing for food
In the rough ground.
Ragged children playing.
A primitive but peaceful scene
Of eternal life in the desert,
Unchanged for centuries.
And yet changes are to be seen.
Children in westernised clothes,
Satchels on their backs.
A new generation – eager to learn
The ways of the modern world,
As they wait for transport
To take them to 'modern' schools;
Abandoning a way of life
Unchanged since biblical times ...

BASRA
Iraq 1970

Living in a compound – surrounded by high walls;

Security guards at the gates and wild dogs outside.

From the flat roof of my bungalow

I can see Arab villages,

Primitive huts in the desert;

Barefoot children with beautiful dark eyes,

Ragged but content with their simple

way of life.

Beneath the date palms thin chickens

Scratch for food in the barren ground.

One is always aware of the mysterious

life here.

The howling of dogs as darkness

descends;

The twittering of bulbul birds

As the heat subsides.

These are memories forever retained.

Mysterious – frightening, perhaps!

MEMORIES OF DUBAI

So many memories of wide-open spaces;

Views from my windows of different places.

Deserts and sand-dunes

And roaming camels.

By the creek in ancient Dubai

There is constant noise

Of dhows being mended

And fishing nets repaired.

An occasional quarrel breaks out

among fishermen.

Along the waterfront there is

constant hustle;

Arabs shout, selling their wares.

Strange cattle and goats

Are unloaded from boats.

Horns blare from many cars.

A timeless scene of the old and new.

THOUGHTS OF LIVING

Thoughts from time spent in Basra, Iraq

What is happiness but a few fleeting moments?
To live is to suffer the heights and the depths;
The goodness of people in close relationships –
The warmth of understanding and unity
In speaking the same language.

Awareness of sounds ...
The melancholy drone of a plane
Far, far up in the sky
As it speeds towards a far off place
Its passengers lost in a world of space ...

A train whistles in the distance
And in the strange, mystical country
Of the Middle East
There is always noise.

The Müller calling worshippers to prayer,
At dusk and at dawn.
The twittering of the 'bulbul' birds
As the heat subsides.
Heat seems to emphasise sound ...

The howling of dogs
As darkness descends.
The musical sound of çicadas
And other night-time creatures.

MEMORIES

Walking along a tree-lined road
On a warm summer evening,
Shadows through the trees;
Twittering of birds
As they settle to roost.
Lights shining through open windows.
Suddenly I hear music
A melody so profound
And full of nostalgia
I am transfixed
As my memory takes me back
To long ago!

A DRIVE ACROSS THE DESERT

We left Basra at dawn; a strange trio – a young Chief Accountant, a bearded consultant of late middle age and myself, a middle-aged tutor of a small group of expatriot children. We were all working for an oil company in the Middle East.

We drove into the desert just as the sun was rising, a magnificent orange ball that appeared on the horizon. The road across the desert was precarious because the boulders lining the route to Ur of the Chaldes had been knocked down or smashed during recent conflicts. We saw oases and stray camels. A little further on we met a lone Arab walking to his destination – we offered him a lift, which he declined saying he would arrive at his destination days too early.

A while later, we met another old man riding backwards on a donkey, with an old rug and chickens on its back. We waved to him and continued on our way, eventually arriving in Ur of the Chaldes to find our primitive guesthouse – a decrepit building. We arranged beds for the night and then drove to the desert again to find the Ziggerut, an ancient monument partially restored, for tourism I imagine. We climbed the many steps and, after exploring, surveyed the area to find the reason for this trip ... a large 'dig' to visit the next day.

We returned to the guesthouse to find it invaded by a party of Americans – no doubt 'doing' the Middle East – very noisy and demanding. We were given a meal in an old office and were then shown our sleeping quarters – iron bedsteads in a corridor with broken fly nets and windows as well as the usual noise of barking dogs and general Arabic sounds.

We were up early the next day and, after a rather primitive breakfast – again in the office as the American party had taken over the (cont.)

.... A drive across the desert

area, we packed our belongings and set off for the heart of the desert. This area was well protected by an armed guard. After negotiations with J. who spoke fluent Arabic, the guard got in the car, with his gun pointed at a dangerous angle, with instructions that if anything was removed from the 'pit' we'd be shot. This strange pit or dell was surrounded by a high wall and buried within this wall were caskets or burial coffins - very small and eerie, the remains of queens and nobles no doubt, who were buried with artefacts, jewels and scrolls of many centuries ago.

J and D managed to unearth a few scrolls, unseen by the guard, which was the object of the exercise. We made our way to several mounds on very rough ground where we found bits of pottery and bits of jewellery - I still have a few pieces of pottery.

Eventually we made our way back to the car and bade farewell to the guard who inevitably asked for a tip and was well rewarded; where the scrolls had been hidden one didn't ask.

We made our way out of the area heading for the Baghdad to Basra road for our return journey. It was dusk by this time and beside the road were many small shacks and other dwellings or villages where the animals were tethered at night - goats, sheep, donkeys and the odd thin cattle. As we drove past we could see wisps of smoke coming from the fires and noisy children and barking dogs. It is amazing to experience the sounds and smells of typical Arab village life - so symbolic of Binlicle ... a life of comparative peace and tranquillity, which hasn't changed much over the centuries. Our minds were overcome by the sights and sounds of this ancient land ... now so horribly desecrated by Saddam Hussein's regime.

We found our way back to Basra and the real world from whence we eventually went our separate ways.   The End.

EMOTIONS

To LIVE – is to reach the heights,
With moments of supreme happiness
In finding affinity of body and mind.
The goodness of people in close relationships,
A spiritual awareness of the pattern of living.
A destiny and purpose –
Only momentary flashes ...
To LIVE – is to suffer,
To reach the depths
Of despair and uncertainty,
Of black depression that can so easily
Engulf one's mind.
To LIVE – is to feel,
To be aware of sound and smell,
The beauty and harshness of nature.
An exquisite melody and song of birds ...
The warmth of the sun,
The tenderness of chosen words,
The touch of fingers intertwined.
In these days of rush and tear
Have we forgotten the importance of TOUCH?

MOODS

Few understand the torment of loneliness
The isolation of mind overwhelmed by stress.
You chatter with friends about this and that
But one's soul is really withdrawn and flat.

How hard to keep on an even keel,
When life's uncertainties make us feel
The highs and lows
And all the blows ...

When you've reached the depths of despair,
Knowing that blackness is ever near.
But the black mood passes yet again.
One laughs away the agony and pain!

So one's love of life ...
The warmth of the sun
Removes all the strife
That enveloped one.

So much tenderness in chosen words;
The many sounds, the chorus of birds.
The gentle touch of fingers entwined
As lovers we meet – as lovers, unwind.

CONFLICT

There have always been conflicts

From time immemorial.

Why?

Man's greed and desire for power;

An inability to heed the rules of Nature.

The Natural World has equal power and might

That can never be eliminated

By strength of technology

In this modern age.

Technology cannot change

The conflicts of Natural Phenomena.

The laws of Nature rule supreme ....

Fearful and wonderful

Even in the midst of war.

NIGHT

Living in a wing of an ancestral house in Kent

The lonely hours of the night

When the wind howls;

Windows rattle,

Every sound is eerie and wild;

Imagination as vivid as a child.

The terror of the night

When the world around you

Appears so dark.

Shadows moving –

It's only the curtains blowing.

A dog barks in the distance …

Wild – mournful!

Will the daylight never come

To release one from these

Terrors of the night?

HAPPINESS

Happiness is an illusive quality;
Fleeting moments of awareness and perfection.
Moments to be treasured,
To be envied, perhaps.
Each day to be lived to the full,
For life is so fragile.

But the highs and lows,
The grey periods,
The uncertainties
Of the day to day living
Make for richness
At any age or time.

So much of living is spent in working,
In raising children.
With hopes that _their_ lives
Will bring about continuity …
Of the pattern of living,
In loving and sharing.

A new generation
In a brave new world.
A world so different
As the twentieth century
Nears its end.
A new century and challenge.

TIME—WHAT IS TIME?

We chase it, we mark it.
Sometimes it goes too fast
And at times we lose it.
Time has in elusive quality.
If we allow it, it will rule our lives;
Take over every hour.

Never enough time for the daily round.
Catching our train ...
It's late again!
When we are travelling to far
off places
We gain time, we lose time.

Supposing Big Ben, our
ruler of time,
Closed down for a day, not
even a chime.
Would there be panic
For this loss of time?
Could our body clocks help us to cope?

Sleeping, meal-times, TV and radio,
And no time to guide us, to plan our time ...
Oh! What fun it would be to lose time for a day!

WAITING ... A GIFT OF TIME

Waiting – always waiting.
Waiting at a bus stop;
Queuing at a shop.
It has become a habit
And no one ever queries it.

Waiting for the doctor,
He's nearly always late ...
So many patients, so little time.
He comes when the food
Is served on the plate.

Getting to the airport
Afraid of being late.
Waiting at the check-in;
Then waiting for our flight
We queue at the gate.

At last we're on the plane
So now we're on our way.
No, again there's some delay.
Waiting for the runway to be free;
And then, oh joy, we're on our way.

There's justice in this waiting
There's time to consider.
There's beauty in contemplation
Of the world around us
And this fragile life.

A STRANGER FROM AFAR

A new arrival in a strange city;
Walking along the lonely streets,
Seeing new places,
Meeting new faces.

Absorbing, discarding ...
Flitting like an insect.
Always I am watching
As people hurry by.

Reaching out –
Yearning for love.
Sometimes a lout
Gives me a shove!

But at the end of the day
One is always alone ...
I must be positive;
There's always tomorrow!

Another day to find my way.

WHERE ARE WE GOING?

To nurture one's soul
We need harmony,
Harmony in nature
To behold the real world -
The cities, the country,
Wide plains and deserts.

But what are we doing?
Where are we going?
E-mail, dot com and web site.
Have we forgotten
The use of our senses?

The gift of vision - of light;
The shapes of trees, of buildings.
To see the beauty of life in a child.
The softness of a baby's skin.
The touch of a hand - a gentle kiss.

The wondrous sound of music
So essential to life.
The sound of birdsong,
Of leaves rustling
On a windy day.

The smell of freshly ground coffee
And newly baked bread;
The scent of flowers.
The feel of velvet
And texture of wood.
The taste of sun-ripened fruit.

These are realities
So essential to life
Not the harshness and noise
Of this modern world.

"Saints leave me cold and martyrs seem lacking in enterprise, but a really attractive sinner can always command my sympathy".
(from a play by Frank Stayton called No Surrender)

SEASONS

Another year nearing its end
Brings memories and feelings,
Some sunshine, some showers,
Much foliage and flowers ...

An intense awareness
Of colour and smell -
Whatever the season,
Whatever the weather.

A freshness and clarity
With the coming of spring;
Sounds of insects and birds
In high summer.

The soaring song of the robin,
The glorious colours of autumn.
Followed by the starkness and beauty
Of a winter's day.

These are the gifts
One must treasure ...
The ability to feel and to see,
To dream, perhaps!

SPRING

War, strife, destruction.

And yet spring is eternal.

Buds open,

Trees burst into new leaf,

Birds sing, seeking a mate.

Springtime heeds not the horror of conflict.

A cleansing and renewal of life,

A feeling of hope for the future.

If only humankind could see it.

"I believe in the stars; I believe they govern this infernal muddle we call the world. If you are born under the wrong kind of star there's nothing doing for you until you go back where you came from and get born again, under the right kind of star".

F.S

SOLITUDE

The clock ticked on.
I lie on the floor,
My mind alert,
My body inert.
I think
Is this the end?
It threatens to
engulf me.
It can't be,
I love life,
There is too much
to live for.
The TV flickers,
As darkness
descends,
Hours go by.
The telephone
rings ......
Suddenly I hear the sound,
A key in the lock,
Help is coming.

IN LIMBO

I know not where I am,
In a life so suddenly changed.
I know not who I am,
Perhaps I'm becoming deranged?
After a turbulent life
Of much travelling and strife,
I thought I'd found a haven
Put down some roots.

But it wasn't to be.
No longer can I flee.
A year or more from pillar to post,
My life in a wheelchair and feeling so lost.
My right side dysfunctional
But my brain still intact!

A restless spirit in an alien world.
But I must go forward
To whatever life holds.

THOUGHTS LYING IN A HOSPITAL BED

I lie in my hospital bed

And let my thoughts drift asunder;

Of mountains, lakes and deserts

And places of great wonder.

So many memories of days gone by

That are still so vivid in my mind's eye.

VIEW FROM MY WINDOW
Highlands

The view from my window

High among trees and shrubs.

A distant glimpse of the river

Seen through pine trees.

A few cottages on the edge of the town.

They say it will change

As summer recedes.

Swirling mists envelop the trees.

A kaleidoscope of colour

As leaves obtain their autumnal hue.

Breathtaking sunsets

As the days grow shorter ...

And winter slows down

The pace of living once again ...

COMING TO TERMS WITH LIFE

To accept one's temperament
And live according to ideals
Instead of adjusting to others;
Inevitably - acting a part
In much of day to day living.

Perhaps it's wiser to submerge
Natural instinct,
And run with the herd
In order to survive.

Thus avoiding the isolation,
The loneliness of mind
When perceptions are too keen ...
One's love of life overwhelming.

It is rare to meet
A fellow human being
With the same perceptions.
A cry in the wilderness.

GOOD FRIDAY

On the cliffs at Dunwich
A carpet of yellow gorse,
The seas grey and infinite.
Fleeting cloud masses ...
Seagulls battle against the wind,
Magnificent in their graceful flight.
A scene so timeless and peaceful
As we meet on Good Friday
At a yearly meeting of friends –
To consume hot-cross buns and coffee.

FREESIAS

The most delicate and powerful of all flowers.

Their perfume permeating the senses,

A blend of colour and structure of bloom

Of such perfection,

A miracle of nature.

A CHANGE OF DIRECTION

It is said that a change of direction is stimulating and the spice of life in order to overcome the humdrumness of daily routine, although to many people routine is security. However, too sudden or great a change can become a roller-coaster, whereby one loses all sense of direction when trying to pick up the threads of one's life and set things in some sort of order... all this went through Jane's mind as she waited for her flight to be called. She had begun to unwind once she had negotiated the usual procedures at the airport and had entered the departure lounge, with a mixture of anticipation and fear.

She had sold her London flat; worked through her month's notice in job as receptionist; said farewell to her few close friends and, having no close relatives, felt she had no obligations to anyone but herself.

"Have you really thought this through?" her friend Diane had asked her.

A year ago, after the death of her boy-friend Clive in a car accident, friends had urged her to 'snap-out' of her despair. "Go on holiday – change your direction and have the courage to start living again," Diane said to her, "Clive wouldn't have liked you to go on grieving!"

Jane arranged her summer leave, having been to a travel agency. "Can you recommend a quiet area, near lakes and mountains, where it is safe to be alone?"

The travel agent assessed this attractive girl; a slender figure with beautiful auburn hair, but her eyes were sad and there was much tenseness in her manner.

"I have just had a cancellation – a quiet hotel in Northern Spain," he said giving her further details. ....(cont.)

..... *A change of direction*

"Thank you, that sounds just what I need and the vacancy fits in with my holiday plans," she said.

She returned to her flat with brochures and details, wondering if she'd got the courage to go off on her own. Two years ago she and Clive had planned just such a holiday.

The short flight and coach drive to her destination was uneventful, reaching the small hotel late in the evening. The view from her window was staggering and, although she felt remote, she was too exhausted to dwell on the past and a sense of excitement entered her being before she fell into a deep sleep – thinking, "Tomorrow, I can't wait for tomorrow!"

She awoke refreshed and hungry but a little shy as she entered the dining room. There were only a few guests, mostly German and French.

"Good morning, Miss Davis. I hope you feel rested?"

Jane glanced briefly at the proprietor, as he served her breakfast, a delicious meal of fruit, croissants and coffee. She was a little surprised to hear an English accent.

"Thank you, yes. Now I'm impatient to start exploring. Can you supply me with suitable maps and directions, please?" Jane asked him.

"With pleasure, but please remember the sun is very powerful from about mid-day, when we have our siesta," he said.

"Thank you, I will remember," Jane replied, before setting off with maps and her camera..... (cont.)

.... A change of direction

After a pleasant morning spent wandering through the village, so typical of Northern Spain, with its Arabic culture of centuries ago – and taking many photographs; she found a small café for her lunch and then returned to the hotel, tired but feeling more contented than for a long time. She spent a lazy afternoon in her room, unwinding, reading and sleeping until it was time to join the other guests for dinner.

As she sipped her coffee Paul, the owner, chatted to the other guests and then sat down at her table.

"May I?" he asked. "I'm curious. Why is an attractive girl like you staying alone?"

"Why is a young Englishman running a small hotel in this remote part of Spain?" she replied. "You seem to work very hard, where are the rest of the staff?"

I cannot get staff in this area," he replied, "especially needed for reception. Pedro, my chef, is exceptional but there is a limit as to how much he can do to help me".

Gradually, a close friendship developed and when there was a rush, Jane offered to help, both in reception and elsewhere.

"Why did you come to Spain?" Jane asked him one day.

"I was tired of the rat-race and living in London. My young wife died after complications with our first infant," he said.

"I'm so sorry – what about the baby?" Jane asked.

.... A change of direction

"My son only lived a few hours. This place has been a haven and I'm learning to live again. Thank you for your sympathy; I haven't talked to anyone about my loss since being here," Paul said.

Jane enjoyed walking around the lakes – also using the hotel swimming-pool and sometimes Paul joined her.

"I have a free evening at the week-end" he said to her, as it became a natural occurrence to share each other's company. "Pedro says he will keep an eye on the few guests. Would you like to have a drive into the hills; I know of a quiet little restaurant run by a colleague".

"I'd like that very much – which evening will that be?" Jane asked.

"The German guests leave on Saturday morning and new arrivals don't come until Sunday," replied Paul. "Be ready at about six o'clock on Saturday".

"Thank you – I'll look forward to an evening away from the hotel with you," said Jane.

As Saturday approached, Jane took extra care with her appearance. She still felt unsure of herself in what seemed to be a growing empathy between them, not having had any relationship since the death of Clive. Nevertheless, she felt a stirring excitement. She dressed casually but took extra care with her make-up and brushed her hair until it shone like gold; when she took a final look at herself in the mirror she was pleased to see how well and relaxed she looked.

Paul was waiting for her as she walked outside to his car. "Oh my! You look beautiful," he said as he opened the car door for her.
They drove through villages and up mountains until they reached a
........(cont.)

.... A change of direction

small restaurant.

"Will this do?" Paul asked. "Carlo is a superb cook."

"Of course!" Jane said, as they parked the car. "What a wonderful view!"

Carlo came out to greet them as they got out of the car.

"Welcome, good to see you Paul, and good evening Madame. Please come inside." It was a romantic setting and Carlo led them to a table looking on to the valley below. He produced the menu and a welcoming drink.

"Is everything to your liking?" Carlo asked, after serving a very special Spanish meal, pouring their wine and bowing graciously.

"Thank you, Carlo. An excellent meal," Paul said and Carlo left them alone to enjoy their meal and each other's company.

"Tell me about yourself, Jane. I still know so little about you, and why you are alone; I'm glad to see you looking less sad. Tell me, please. You must realise I am growing attached to you."

"Like you, Paul," Jane said, "my life was shattered about two years ago – when my fiancé was killed in a car accident. I have tried to submerge all feeling until my friends urged me to take a hold of myself and start living again … and here I am!"

"Thank you for telling me," Paul said, as he lifted his glass to hers, "Here's to us and our futures."

They talked for hours and then drove slowly back to the hotel, both

..... A change of direction

rather overcome by the wine and their growing intimacy - and the exquisite moonlit night.

As they turned into the hotel grounds and stopped the car, Paul said, "Good-night, darling", kissing her gently on the lips, "sleep well".

As the time for her return to England and her job loomed ever closer, Jane and Paul had begun to feel a very close bond and Jane dreaded going back to her old life.

"I hesitate to ask you, after such a short time, but would you like to help me run this hotel? We both seem to have so much in common," Paul asked her, rather nervously.

"Oh! Yes, I don't know ... please let me think about it." Jane said, as she prepared for her return journey. She realised they were both falling in love but still felt a little apprehensive at the prospect of 'starting again'.

"Was it fate or providence or whatever - that guided me here. Was the travel agent cupid in disguise?" Jane thought, as he left the hotel for her journey back to England.

Paul telephoned her nearly every day - awaiting her answer.

And here she was ..... on her way to starting an exciting new life!

The End.

CHILDREN
(To all the children I have helped, collectively and individually especially with dyslexia)

So many children, countries, and far off lands.

From the Middle East, both south and north,

Ex-patriots of various ages

All needing help at different stages.

Work was hard but we had fun;

Seeking fauna in the sun.

So many children ... for so many years

I've guided and helped to overcome fears,

Lost in a maze of numbers and letters,

Seemingly caught in chains and fetters.

Encouraging confidence and hope

That they would understand and cope,

As words and numbers began to make sense ...

We had fun!

What has happened to these many children?

From tinies to adults, both here and there.

I hope that life has brought them good cheer.

MY CHILDREN

My three children, so diverse in nature;
My daughter, the eldest, born under Aquarius,
Inclined to dream and be self absorbed,
She loved excitement and was never bored,
Her passion was dancing and make-believe.

My elder son, a typical Scorpio,
Impatient, but creative and organised.
My right-hand man from an early age
But who so often flew into rage.
He was, even so, a gentle soul.

My younger son, quite the reverse,
Strong-willed and so often perverse.
Left-handed and meticulous.
An introvert and much of a loner ...
Deep thinking and a rather late talker.

Life was hard for us all, but they weren't bored...
They made wonderful villages in the soil
Which lasted for many weeks of endless toil.
Their model railways absorbed for hours
They cared for their pets and played with their cars.

As the sole parent and teaching all day
I had to be strong and in control ...
To give them security and love
Each so different as they grew up.
But was I a good mother?

One will never know

BEAR

I am a Canadian bear with a lovely green bow. I am large and white and very cuddly. I belonged to my dear friend Mark.

One very cold winter, his grandma came to stay. A few days later she slipped on freezing rain and broke her wrist, so Mark gave me to her to cuddle.

I was put in her luggage and we flew back to England. I became loved by her friends and relations. My lady made several more flights and left me to guard her home.

A few years later, we went to Canada to live. This time I was packed in a crate and transported by sea. It was a long journey.

I was happy to be among my old friends, and cats and this time I had pride of place on my lady's bed.

One year later it was necessary to return to England once again. I was packed in a crate with cushions and treasures and the journey took about a month.

We stayed in a small flat in Kent for nearly a year and then we moved to a flat in Suffolk. I sat on my lady's comfortable bed and was often used to rest her head when reading in bed at night time.

Such peace wasn't to last. My lady had a sudden right-sided stroke. She was taken to hospital where she stayed for nearly four months.

……(cont.)

BEAR

Amongst the many cards and flowers she was given, was a small brown teddy bear, adorned with rosebuds – and loved by all the nurses as well as my lady – and me!

My lady was unable to return to her newly furnished flat and had to move to a residential home nearby, which had a beautiful view.

By this time, I was beginning to feel rather tired and jaded. The carers took pity on me late at night and offered to put me through the washing process.

Early the next morning, one of the carers took me back to my lady's room, saying, "He's nice and clean, but a little dizzy". My green bow was sparkling too.

I now sit on my lady's bed with my friend the brown bear close beside me and the staff always see that we sit on the cushions together.

The End.

REINCARNATION

I think I'd like to be a cat;
To be well fed but not too fat.
My masters must be cultured, wealthy
And, of course, extremely healthy.

Cooking and eating the finest of fare,
With titbits for me, so tasty and rare.
I'd dream about my ill-spent youth;
Few would know the real truth.

Of my howling and prowling,
Of my chasing and wooing
The beauteous females
With long, lustrous tails.

I would like to feel that my seed
Would continue my fine breed
For generations to come.
Wise, proud and so handsome,

Like me!

Quotes from a play called "Laurels"

"I believe nature loves us, if we are kind to the birds and the animals and if we appreciate her manifestations; I believe she tries to advise us through wonderful sunsets and colour schemes, the washing of the waves on the shore and the murmur of the river."

F.S

BLACKOUT

January 1999

Relaxing, reading, watching TV,
Suddenly total blackness.
I pull the curtains back ...

Total blackness in the street outside.
I struggle to find the doorway
Remember a torch in the hall.

It needs a new battery ...
I find matches and Christmas candles,
Light several and place them in holders.

I phone my daughter in Sandy Lane;
"Have you a power-cut?"
"No".. we chat for a while.

She phones a friend in Melton:
"Have you a power-cut?"
"No, have you?" "No"!

They realise the absurdity of their conversation
with much laughter.
Darkness continues –

No hot drink, no warm bed.
I try to remember what lights had been on.
Decide to go to bed—by candlelight.

Much later the lights come on;
Get out of bed to check the lights...
And make a much needed hot drink.

Page 54

FINDING THE WAY

Sometimes we take the wrong turning,
Turn to the left instead of the right.
The road is rough and twisting …
With many hidden dangers.
Storm clouds gather and we feel so lost …
We turn a corner, go round a bend;
Fearful that this could be the end.
Suddenly we see a faint light,
As we get nearer it seems very bright,
The light fades and reason takes hold,
Positive thought once more we behold.
We veer to the right and know it's the way
To meet the challenges of each new day.
The ups and downs that are part of life;
The highs and lows and moments of strife.
Waiting and wondering what comes next?

"Life is so strange ... today is always real while yesterday seems a thousand years ago and tomorrow is just a remote possibility".

F.S

PHILOSOPHIES OF LIVING—BEING

There are many colours
Between black and white;
Colours of the universe,
The colours of life itself,
If only we could see them.

But many, having a one-track mind,
Whose outlook makes them all but blind …
Blind to the frailties of humankind;
Whilst loving – giving, forgetful of self
Are greater riches than pursuit of wealth.

Preconception of people and places,
Envy of others and dreaming of dreams …
Is an escape from reality
Unseeing beyond infinity.

The greatest gift is awareness of soul …
Of having an aim and reaching one's goal …
We all have a purpose in life
However great the struggle and strife.

"The original egotist was the man who praised God for having made him and promptly invented the devil to excuse his sins"
F.S

Previously Published Poems
By Helen Stayton Persse

Conflict' (from Straight from the Heart,)

United Press

'Reflections' (from Straight from the Heart,)

United Press

'Seasons' (from Straight from the Heart,)

United Press

'Happiness' (from A Way of Life,)

Poetry Now

'A Cottage in the Country' Eastern England,

Poetry Now

'My Children' (So Starts a New Beginning)

Poetry Now

'Moods' (from Captured in Rhyme)

Triumph House

'Mystery of Life' (With Peace on Earth)

Triumph House

'Reincarnation' (A Picture of Rhyme)

Triumph House

'Happiness' (Burning Emotions)

Anchor Books

'Time' (Changing Emotions)

Anchor Books

'Emotions' (Whispers in the Garden)

Poetry Guild

'Emotions'

International Society of Poets

Why not give a copy of ***Episodes of Living*** as a gift to your friends! Check your local bookstore or order here.

Number of Copies _____ Price _____ Currency _____ Sub Total _____

Shipping & Handling   _____

Total Order   _____

Name _____

Address _____

City _____

County/Province/State _____

Postal/Zip Code _____

Country _____

Telephone _____

Email _____

Fax. _____

Credit Card: _Amex   Visa   Master Card

☐   ☐   ☐

Number: _____ Exp. Date _____

Signature _____

Please visit www.staytonpublishing.com
Email: staytonpublishing@earthlink.net

Order in United Kingdom   Order in Canada/US

Fax Number: 01.394.384.548   Fax Number: 416.489.1684
Delivery: £2.50   Delivery: $4.00
Retail Price: *£10.50 GBP*   *Retail Price:* *$21.50 CDN*